If I tell you that even the moon writes
when you
Singing th
As they gı
harmony.

CW01500561

The folktɑ
Are storie
From her journal with the secrets of
space
Weaving myths and legends again.

The glowing words she wrote and read
Whirled around the night skies
And with stars as her quill, writing tales
Enchanting the world in lunar glaze.

A crescent or a glimmering orb of white
light
And as she writes, the worlds collide
A cosmic prose, a celestial chronicle
divine
The constellations are proof, even the
moon writes.

People die, but grief doesn't.
It lingers by the door, flowing in every
time you open it.
It's often too heavy, rupturing its way
through the postern.
Grief follows you out into the world.
It stays with you as you lie in the arms
of Morpheus, warbling a soft lullaby.
Grief pecks you on the cheek every time
you wake up.
It's present in the air you breathe,
enters your lungs, and augments.
It grows like ivy around your heart,
clinging tightly.
Till it asphyxiates you, strangles your
center.
And all you're left with is blood and
grief.
Because grief stays; it doesn't leave.
It's present in the coffee you drink in
the morning,
In the back pocket of your jeans,
In the diary you carry with you.
Grief is everywhere, even when love
isn't.
Hold onto it, but don't make it a part of
you.

And when it finally gets too heavy, open
your hand, let it go.
But don't open the windows just yet.
Remember, grief never leaves. It lingers.

———————————————

Can I really blame you for leaving after I
kicked you out?
Is it your fault that you left when I told
you to leave?
Your warmth was too hot for me; it
burned my skin,
so I put it out and let it rot with gloom.

I scream and I yell, and I push you out
the door.
I keep calling your name as I lay hurting
on the floor.
You stayed for so long, with your back
against my door.
You knocked so hard, asked me
questions, begged for more.
But my heart couldn't risk opening up
anymore.

I miss you, your voice, but you can't
know
the site of all the punctures in my weary
heart
and all the perpetrators that pierced it
and speared and tore it apart.

You're not staunch enough to handle
the rainfall of arrows
that strike and slaughter people down
to the core.
I'm not indestructible enough to divert
the storm towards you
or to stand up and stand tall all on my
own.

Who is to be held accountable for the
blood that's on my hands?
Who should be held responsible for the
gore as it flows down into the abyss?
Can I place the blame on the part of me
that died?
Can I feel guilt for the part of me that
died?

I have questions that don't have any
answers.
I have problems that have no solutions.
My mere existence is an enigma to me.
*Please be waiting at the other side of
the door for me.*

Hey, I know I make you the villain in
every poem I write.
Hey, I know they blame you for our last
fight.
I've told the world about it a thousand
times;
even for me, it's hard to believe it
sometimes.

But when you love someone too little,
they leave you; everyone knows this.
But when you love someone too much,
they stop loving you; they get tired of
you.
Now this, not a lot of people know.

You'd be wondering now
how to love someone the perfect
amount,
how to know they'll stay without any
doubt.
You can't love someone the perfect
amount
because perfect isn't constant.

For me, holding your hand while we
walk under the stars

or listening to you talk about your
crappy day in our car,
that was perfect; for me, it was
everything.
For you, however, it was something.
You liked it at first, then you grew tired
of it,
like a four-year-old gets tired of his two-
days-ago-bought toy.
But he has to pretend to like it
because of the way he got it,
by throwing a tantrum in the middle of
the store.
But now he doesn't like it anymore.
No one blames the kid; he's just a child.
But that excuse couldn't work for you.

Now I'm rethinking it again: are you to
blame for this,
or was it me, thinking I could have
something nice in the first place?

———————————————

I wrote a thousand letters,
telling you about every atom of my
being
and how they all align and excite every
time you're near.
And I addressed all those letters to your
mailbox and burnt them,
never posted them, hoping that you'll
detect the love impulses my heart sends
out.
Crawling to you because the love my
heart holds is too weak for my body
to stand straight and find solace
in the comforts of any other arms than
yours.

To love is to endure the distress.
To love is to observe the pattern.
To love is to swallow the storm.

The air seems to be taking heavy sighs
today.
The sun is still, refusing to rise.
The trees stand scared, cloaked in
defeat;
the paths I wander are veiled in
shadows.

It seems the weather calls out to me,
to take up my notebook and write a
poem.
The moon, too, wears a veil of
melancholy,
as the ocean waves are still—no sound.

I pick up my quill, dipping it in the ink.
With quivering hands, I write your
name,
For I could not have written a *sadder
poem.*

The dirt beneath my feet felt harder
than before.
I took the shovel out and started
digging,
only to find my childhood buried in a
box—
a time capsule, a box of souvenirs.

I take out the seeds and plant them
with my hands,
and they grow each time it rains from
my eyes.
But the flowers do not bloom; only the
thorns grow,
and a new memory comes before my
eyes.

And I weep again; I weep for the
childhood that I lost,
that I buried beneath,
that now pricks my feet
every time I walk down memory lane.

―――――――――――――――――

Do you think the baby bird that got lost
grew up with a hole in its heart?
Do you think the mother bird that lost
her nest kept searching until she tore
the tree apart?
Did the child ever feel love?
Did the mother ever learn how to love?
Was it part of fate or some divine
intervention?
Did the child ever fly, or did it just crawl
in search of something to keep its little
heart warm?
And when they met again—by accident
or intent—
Were the questions ever asked?
Were the answers ever given?
Did nature itself intervene, confess its
guilt?
Or did the hatred grow so strong, like
ivy around their hearts?
Did hope remain, or was it shattered at
first sight?

I've loved the fire all my life.
At one point, I thought I could control it
—

make it flicker and dance with my eyes.
To have the fire under my control was
my dream,
until I realized it was the power I craved
—

to let the world burn around me but
remain untouched.

A child with all smiles doesn't conform
to this world,
so they broke my teeth to match the
worst.
And then, one day, they said I was too
mature,
but I was the only one who knew
it's called being insecure.

January, you were supposed to pick me
up
& dust me off,
wipe away the drops of agony imprinted
on my cheeks.
Instead, you come erupting in from the
front door,
like an angry father—
half-empty bottle in one hand, a fist in
the other,
striking everything that comes in his
way to the ground.
And I sit and wonder if the nuclear
bomb is made up of drunk fathers.

January, there is a cavity where your
heart was supposed to be,
so I try to pour love down that void,
but it turns into nothingness.
It is hard to travel to space, so if I ever
wish to view the black hole,
I'll know where to look for it—
in my father's chest.

January, you promised me a fresh start,
but you mercilessly pour the vessel of
memories down my oesophagus,

as I sit gasping and gulping, accepting
my defeat.
January and my father are the same.
Please don't let February be my mother.

How the mansion was pulverized,
leaving behind only echoes of *"home."*
Even a fortress goes to rack and ruin
if it's made to bear the heat.
Who's to blame for all the calamity that
was caused?
How did all the fingers end up pointed
at me?
But I'll take the blame and wear it like a
medal around my neck
if it means protecting you from all the
stones they'd throw.
I'll act as a barricade in front of you,
and I'll gladly be stoned to death.

The worst part of love is the betrayal,
when the person you love the most puts
a gun to your head.
And all your life, you thought death
would come in the form of a Grim
Reaper.
You had never thought that Death could
be so beautiful.
Your mind starts searching for what
went wrong; how the fungus crawled
into your airtight container
or how the pests managed to ruin
something so graceful.
It's that time that you realize it doesn't
matter if they pull the trigger or not;
you're dead either way, but you're glad.
A life that started from the moment you
laid eyes on them ends the same way
you wanted it to—
looking in their eyes,
a master in the art of treachery.
A building built on a rotten foundation
is bound to collapse.

There may have been a moment
where I was loved by you,
but I loved better than you.
I was so convinced that I was unlovable.
I wanted the world to know my scars,
my history, my pain, my past.
You loved me, and I thought you
mocked me.
You didn't care if they'd crucify you for
it.
I was never a part of your world.
I could never be a part of your world—
I was against everything you believed in,
an abandoned faith.

And then the sun set;
it got scary again.
Nothing ever lasts, but nothing ever
changes either.
I'll be in the dark till the light comes in,
but I'll never let it in.
I closed the doors real tight.
I was dethroned; my words had no
meaning anymore.
The curtains dropped; silence spread
everywhere.

The mouth that wanted to scream got
tied up.
No noise—let the intensity of my eyes
preach.
I was given a pen and page and ordered
to write a death sentence—
my death sentence, *our death sentence.*
I could never be enough, in anything,
ever.
All I ever wanted was to be enough—
for once, for someone.

—————————————

When will I drop the knife in my hand?
When will I stop stabbing myself?
The knife with blood dripping down
from it,
the knife that keeps stabbing the same
heart over and over again.
My blood is black, but it's mixed with
red.
My brain hurts; you're still in my head.
When will you truly leave me?
Or when will you become you again?
Or maybe you can stay in my heart just
a little longer
Or maybe I am in love with the way you
hurt me.
I can't touch you; you're just my
memory—
a precious one, just like gold in a cave of
coal.
If I see even just a tear in your glittering
eyes,
I'll tear the entire world apart, rip out
my soul.
Do I want you to go, or do I want you to
stay?
I want you to be happy wherever you
stay.

Every time I think of you, I feel my heart
burst.
It screams internally: is my heart
cursed?
Stay in my heart and follow me
everywhere;
maybe we'll walk into each other
somewhere.
I should hold onto this knife a little bit
longer;
I should linger in this pain a while
longer.
If you must go, then let your memory
linger,
for I'll hold onto the love we shared,
in silence.

November holds me by the throat,
suffocating me with its gray sadness.

November grips my arms with its cold
hands;
November amuses itself as I tremble.

Why is November so cruel to me?
How can time be so brutal, barbaric?

November echoes, dreams that once
were hopes;
memories linger as teardrops fall to the
ground.

November's wind carries a melancholic
melody;
November sighs, breaking its promise of
a peaceful time.

November dims the colorful and lively
sky;
November silences the trees and their
silent cries.

November digs up the graveyard of
all the emotions I've buried this year.

November keeps me in the dark;
November finds it entertaining as I fall.

A year ago, sorrow lingered as
November came to a close.
Yet this year, joy blooms as November
departs.

I'll never feel whole again;
a part of me will always be with you.
Unlike a worm, I won't be able to
regenerate.
Would you come back before it's too
late?
Drowning in the pool of my own tears,
staring as reality weighs down on me.
I'll have to row the boat alone or jump
off,
and I'll have to shed my skin like a snake
to rid myself of you, along with all this
filth
they call love.

You knew you loved the colour pink
till they taught you it's not your thing.
You view the world in a darker shade,
you see the world as it is made.

While the kids thought the tooth fairy
was kind,
you'd never let anyone else roll the dice.
While the kids fought for the princess's
role,
you'd gladly accept the wicked witch's
throne.

You knew you had to bite, claw, and
clench
to make your way through the burning
maze.
You knew you had to keep one hand on
the sword
to fight the battle on your own accord.

You knew you'd make it out alive,
but there was one thing you sacrificed.
Is a human even human without a
heart?
Is an artist even an artist without their
art?

It took me years to look under the bed,
only to find what seemed like a safety
net—
a place for you to fall, a guaranteed
'another shot,'
all while my bed was burning hot.

You don't get to pull the safety pin
of the grenade you've been carrying
and then be astounded as it explodes,
and everything we've built flies apart,
even though you knew my lifeless, weak
heart.

And what's gone is gone; there is no
spare part.
You don't get to know the code,
you don't get the time to reload.

The cruise ship of our love is sinking,
the bomb made of my rage is ticking.
And when it finally detonates,
in its fiery glow, your death awaits.

I am indeed a hopeless creature,
unaware of what to do, how to do.
I want death more than I want life,
but I will fight for breaths if I were
drowning.
I don't want death the same way I'm
living-
drowning in my thoughts; a pool of
regret.
Every second of my life, a fool of life.
But I won't hesitate if you put a gun to
my head
& end my misery, shoot me dead.
I am of no good; I am a lost cause.
Blow away my brains and end its wars.
Every day, I am at war with myself,
a war between my head and my heart.
It's too late now, I'm too scarred,
but it would've been lovely to know
how to live without constant sorrow.

It's been a while since I wrote
something.
My pen mocks me every time I look at
it.
I feel the pages laughing at me, at my
deceit.

"Do you think your words will make the
world a better place?" they ask.
"Do you think your sentences will heal
your inner wounds?" they ask.

I tell them it is not true.
I do not believe in this.
I remind them: I write to remain sane.
I write because writing does not
demand perfection.
I write because it is somehow better
than self-destruction.

I had a choice between a blade or a
pen.
I chose the pen. I don't write every day
—so what then?

What I write does not judge me,
yet the lies are dancing around me.

The best way to die is neither of them.
I could either be the writer or the muse.
I have a way with words, though I may
not be romantic.

I write for the sake of being a person in
this world.
I write so I can be something, to give
something to this world.

People say love is beautiful.
They say it's magical, colourful.
I find love to be scary—
black and white, or gray.

Because it never ends, it never dies.
Being in love is like being a prisoner—
a prisoner who misses his jail,
the place where he starved,
the place of his torture,
the place of his solitude.

Or like that moment when a person is
drowning,
and there are people around him,
but no one can save him.

They all watch as he fights for himself,
and goes down and down,
until there is nothing of him left—
nothing but his memories.

I correct myself:
That is how being in love feels
when it's one-sided.

"I will make you better."
You run towards me, you stab me in the
chest, you tear it open, you dig in, you
take out my heart.
"I found it."
And you cut it-and it's empty.
"No, no, where is your pain?"
You become restless.
You crack open my skull-empty.
"This is not possible."
You take out all my organs.
You know you've lost.
You look me in the eyes,
and I smile as I let my tears run.
You touch them-it burns your hand.
But time has passed now.
I close my eyes, and you beg me to
open them.
"They never know where to look," I
whisper,
as I take my last breath.

"What happened?"

I don't like this question.
So many things have happened—
my stars collided, my planets burst,
my universe vanished, my sun burned.

But my moon's still here.
My moon is still in front of me.

You ask me what happened.
You demand the keys to my dungeon.

You cannot go there; I do not want you
to go there.
It's scary and dangerous, with weird
monsters.
It's my entire past, for god's sake.

You go there, and you don't come back.
So I swallow the keys to the dungeon,
and you leave.
And I watch you go.

"Nothing happened."

And I wonder what was easier—
letting you go or letting you in.

"How are you?"
How am I? I don't know.

I have a black hole in my chest.
I'm often in the depths of my misery.
I'm always drowning in the pool of my
regrets.

I'm in another dimension.
I conquered time; I failed love.
I'm with you, I'm not with you.
I'm in a cave with a monster.
I'm in a cage—I am the monster.

I'm lost in the Mariana Trench.
I've reached my limit; I'm nowhere near
my goal.
I've touched the sky, and I've come
back.
I've seen heaven, and I live in hell.

I've been dead a long time.
I've been alive since the start.
I've eaten, and I've been eaten.
I've swallowed the lumps, and I've cut
them open.

I have a void that can never be filled.
I've not given up; I've been defeated.
I know the end; I'm so naive.

"I'm fine."

"What are you thinking?"
You don't want to know.

I look in your eyes; I want to tell you.
But I can't, because of the gun pointed
at me.

I've been counting days, counting time.
I hear the clock tick every night.

I was thinking about the easiest way
out-
strangle myself with my fears, or drown
myself in my endless tears,
or I could poison myself with the
thought of losing you, of never seeing
you again, of never calling you mine
again.
But it's too much work, and I am tired.

"Nothing."

How did I survive this long?
Fighting and faking war,
giving all hope away,
ending it all again.

You put a gun to my head, and I don't
flinch.
You shatter my glass, crumble my walls,
and I don't blink.
You gave me a bouquet of roses, and I
hold them by the thorns.
I look at you as blood rushes between.
I clench my fist and let it bleed.

Life passes by, and I feel like a con artist,
playing different roles in my own life.

Nothing ever ends; it lingers by a
thread,
sharp enough to cut deep.

To live without dying,
to love without doubting,
to go on empty-handed, empty-minded
is something I might never know, never
feel.

Red

When it all starts—the shooting pain
that comes with it,
and then the moment of weakness as
you hold yourself,
waiting for it to pass, or for it to happen
all over again.

Blue

And then purple, as you sit and tremble,
signaling your mind to force your
zygomaticus major,
pulling the sleeve a little closer to your
hand,
blinking too fast and breathing too slow.

Black

Sits and mocks, a reminder of your
terrible fate
and your lack of control over your mind
—
a scar to prove you were there, and you
couldn't stop.

Green

Or yellow, a chance to try again—

to live through the torment, to sit
through the affliction,
to struggle, to care, and to be fine
again.

Skin
The last resort—
the end of a vacation or the start of
another journey,
a cycle to end or a chance to relapse,
a perfect temptation or a chance for
redemption.

The day you wanted to sever the ties
that bind us,
I stood there—a frozen statue made of
clay,
knowing well the heat was high that
day,
leaving me weak and destructible, an
easy prey.

How can I walk down the path that
leads me away from you?
How did your legs possess the strength
to depart from my side?
So I count the seconds of the hours as
they go by
and wonder what would've happened if
you were by my side.

You came in front of me
with love in your hands.
You tossed it around and showed me
tricks—
Your love for me was like chasing a
butterfly.

I stumbled down running,
I hurt myself again,
but the beauty of your love kept me
going and going.
I bruised and scarred,
but all is fair in love and war.

I gave my attention to you
like a dog does with a ball—
I was ready to do anything.

So I gave you my heart.
I wanted it to be filled with love.
I wanted to drown in it.
I wanted it to burst open.
I wanted to see it red.

You held my heart out,
you checked it all out.
It was heavy with all the pain,

so you dropped it down.

A heart filled with burden
cannot be filled with anything.
Even if you pour something,
a broken heart keeps leaking.

You watered my anxiety—
you helped it grow whole.
Now it has consumed me—
my entire body and soul.
I've heard that not every pain has
meaning.
I give my pain a name; I invite her in; I
show her hospitality.
I pray it'll go easy on me—it preys on
my fragile memories.

My pain is all the colors in the world.
It starts with all the colors in the world,
and they mix together,
blending right into my hollow cavities.

Like a child playing with clay, it merges
together,
forming a large clump of nothing but
darkness.

All I'm left with is black.

Staring at the blinking cursor,
wondering if it's even worth writing
about—
if the pain really needs to be
documented,
if the pain really needs a home.

Pain is the closest thing we know that
can shape-shift,
comes in many forms, yet has a single
purpose.
And still, we decorate it; we keep it
close.

Pain is the start of life and the end of it.

The hardest thing I have ever had to do
is love you so much but show you only
half of it,
because I had to love you in silence.
I showed you enough—not too little for
you to leave,
not too much for you to leave.

I love you more than you love me.
I could go on and on about you;
you'd talk about me for maybe an hour.
I could stare at you forever;
you'd move your eyes away after the
first blink.

I'll never be the first to let go of your
hand;
you get annoyed if I hold it too long.
I could name everything you love;
you could name the top three things I
love.

You'll always be first on my list.
You expect me to come to you every
time,
and I crawl to you every time.

If I were to die, I know you'd cry a little,
maybe be miserable for a week.
If you were to die—no, I'd never let that
happen.

I'd shake the world, I'd go crazy,
and I'd reunite with you somehow.
I can't even imagine it.
I will never write about it.

I've torn myself apart again and again
for nothing; it was all for nothing.
The kind of woman that I am
is the kind you fear more, love less.

I am not the sunset, or the sunrise, or
the night sky;
I am a clear blue sky.
I am not love at first sight.

So I try, and I try hard,
for you to love me,
for you to stay;
for you to love me truly.

I have some good days,
but the nights are all mine.
I don't remember the last time I went to
sleep
with a clear mind, without pain in my
heart.

I scratch my skin so I can take it off,
leave the house without dealing with
who I'm too scared to look at in the
mirror.
I know I'll see my biggest hater,

and I'll want to punch her, choke her,
and end her.
I stay busy; I do not let myself feel.
Why am I her? I could've been someone
else.
I spray perfume all over myself;
I hate it, I loathe myself.
I smell like failure.

I am invisible, and it kills me.
When I am visible, it also kills me.

I could've been cured in my early years;
children and hatred don't go well
together.
I am on the last stage now;
I am on my last edge now.

When I fell off the hill, I saw everyone
who pushed me:
it was her, the woman who made me
and feeds me and says she loves me;
the people who adored me,
the friends who played with me,
the brother who was supposed to
protect me,
and the father—always the father.

I met her in July, an average day.
It wasn't an average day by the end of
it.
The air was cooler near her;
sparkles flew in her wake.
When I thought I could only feel blue,
she made me feel colors I'd never felt
before.

Flowers grow on the paths she walks;
she makes me smile every time she
talks.
The devil greets her with the utmost
respect;
with her presence, my life has a special
effect.

Everything is brighter when she's
around;
everything has meaning when she's
around.
The demons in me stop fighting each
other
every time she tells me she loves me.

She's the kind of kid who'd draw the sun

in the corner of the page, with shades
on.
She's my kind of person.

If all the flowers in the world
start wilting and dying,
if the Earth suddenly stops rotating,
or if the moonlight dims,
let the entire world know
it's because she's sad.

Being in love with her isn't like my
prison;
being in love with her is like walking
barefoot
in a field of lavender.

Maybe I cannot make it in my life,
but I can make her happy in hers.

The words "I'd die for you" mean
nothing anymore,
Because dying is not a punishment
anymore.
It is a way out, a back door.
Dying is a blessing, an end to all
hardships.
I'd die for anybody; what makes you
special?
Death is easy; living the life of cruel
destiny is hard.
What makes you special is that I'd live
for you.
If I had a chance to die, I'd take it
without thinking,
But for you, I'd give it a second thought.
If you tell me not to die, I'd send the
angel away.
If you tell me not to die, I'd crawl out of
my grave.
If you tell me not to die,
I'd bribe whoever deals with death.
If you tell me to come back to you,
I'd leave heaven and come back for you,
Because I love you,
And I'd die and live for you.
Because I love you

To death and to life.

Writing a letter; it's old school, I know,
Finally giving you the apology I owe
To the person who broke my heart,
Or to the one who tore this thing apart.
This thing, the one we had together—
It's autumn, the perfect weather.
Seasons will come, and they'll pass;
I thought what we had was going to
last.
I'm sorry for loving you the way I did;
Never will I ever love again—God forbid.
And you said we could be friends again.
What if I could never move on? What
then?

Now I hear you're with someone else—
She's like a cherry on top in a red dress.
Does she turn every time the door
opens?
Does she write eleven hundred poems?
Are you the reason she can't sleep at
night?
Does she stay quiet, always lets you be
right?
Is she afraid to lose you too,
Or does she still need more clues?

I shouldn't be the one writing this
letter;
She shouldn't be with you—she
deserves better.
You're not the right person, but then
again, who is?
I won't let you paint her heart only to
throw it.
I'll speak up; I'll do something about it.
The hell with this letter—where is the
lighter?

Once I woke up from a really long sleep
To find you nowhere beside me.
I look around and there is no soul,
Just a wide, far-stretched land.
I whisper your name,
And a foreshock occurs; the ground
trembles.
I stand firm; I call out your name,
And I feel the ocean waves rising,
almost as though they will engulf me.
So I call out your name a little louder
than before,
And the sky thunders; the sun starts
coming towards me.
The hurricanes, the thunderstorms, the
earthquakes, and the explosions
All begin right at the moment I say your
name.
So I call out your name once again; this
time I shout it, I scream.
And that beacon of light collapses with
the land,
And it all bursts into this spiraling storm.
Then a universe is created, my universe
—

That's how the *Big Bang* happened.
I have a habit of leaving,

When people start tearing their flesh
apart,
And revealing the monsters inside.
I keep the ugly side to myself;
I'll keep the monsters to myself;
I'll let the fire burn inside me.

*To be loved is to let someone rip you
apart.*
To be loved is to let them enter the cave.
To be loved is to watch till they find it.
*To be loved is to let them heal your
wounds.*

I ask you, who do you love the most in
this world,
And I watch as you dive into your mind,
Opening every door in the palace of
your thoughts.
You open abandoned chests, find
bottles long gone.
You rummage through the dusty
corridors of your memories,
Digging up on the wrong ground
You keep searching in the wrong place,
Naming a thousand people who did
little things—
Things that linger in your memory.
In every room you go through, you find
old photographs
But none of them hold the face you
seek so bad.

Then you ask me the same question,
Little do you know love slips through
the cracks of my mind.
Leaking into my eyes as they search for
you.
And I smile, looking into your eyes,
knowing well:

Every door I open in my mind leads me back to you.

I don't have to write to make you feel
loved.
I don't need to rhyme to convey my
affection, my beloved.
Lines don't have to rhyme to be called
poetry.
Feelings don't have to be reciprocated
for it to be called love.
It's an inferno that burns regardless,
rising high and above.
Look at the sun—an eternal pledge of
undying love.
If you hold my hand, all you'll feel is
love.
Look around you, all you'll see is love.

Love is what remains after a fire.
Love is what carves the stones in the
ground.

You know it's bad when you have to
blink too fast
And move your eyes down, hiding your
weakest side.
Stay silent; you can't risk your breaking
voice,
All while the sky falls from your guileless
eyes.

From the start, you were taught that
crying was for the weak,
Yet, in the end, you were still just a child
with too much prolactin,
With eyes always ready to shed tears,
And a heart always ready to sink deep.

You'd cry in the bathroom for no more
than ten minutes
And come out with a smile, so they
don't doubt your worth,
All while your fists ache from pounding
the bathroom tiles.
But your parents will get a daughter
with all smiles,
The act you've put on from the very first
day.

It's hard to break character, even when
you're not pretending,
And you worry that the tears you always
kept in,
The vault may overflow, echoing the
battles you've fought.

———————————————

How many different words can I use to
explain my damaged heart?
I wonder how long I can repeat
something
Until it is no longer heard anymore,
Until it's nothing; until it loses its
meaning.
How many words can my heart endure
Until it lays down; until it surrenders to
the horrors?
The wall I construct from little strings of
hope
Fails and falls every time you speak.
How long can I keep starting over from
scratch?
How long can I keep piercing myself?
I close my eyes and envision myself,
Sometimes falling off a cliff, crashing
somewhere else.
Sometimes giving up, designing my
grave.
Sometimes fate shows me mercy and
does the dirty work itself.
Am I not meant to be here?
Is there another world somewhere,
Somewhere I can fit in, somewhere I
can be just a person?

A normal life, a normal mind, a normal family.
Can someone ever look at me and see me?
Can I ever be something more than a crestfallen, disappointed, despondent person?

Dear March,
The month of sorrow.
I expected you to be a bed of roses,
After February's torment.
March, you ended up a bed of thorns,
And my tired flesh toppled onto you.
Thirty-one thorns perforated my body,
And I sit, taking one out every day,
Plucking it out and covering the wounds
With bandages made of unfulfilled
promises.
They say that the pain of March will end
once all the thorns are out,
But the scars of March will remain for
eternity.
March, you left me feeble and pale;
You dimmed my gallantry and
suppressed my hopes.
I lay my armor at your feet and concede
my defeat.
I give in to your pummelings and only
crave what they call pity.
As I walk toward April, hoping it will
befriend my worn-out soul.

Midnight, out on the street
Listening to Taylor Swift on repeat
It was raining, lightning flashing across
the skies,
With this constant ache in my chest,
Which grows every time "All Too Well"
plays.
But I don't think you remember it at all;
You wouldn't have gone if you did.
You wouldn't have dragged my heart all
over the place;
You wouldn't have chained it, and you
wouldn't have stepped on it.
Unintentionally the first time,
Intentionally all the other times.
You knew what you were doing.
It hurts so much; you'll never know how
it feels.
To prevent myself from writing your
name in this poem,
To place all the blame on you,
To curse you, to tell the Moon about
you,
To complain to my dog about you—
Every time he barks when the door
opens,
Hoping it's you with his favorite treat,

Hoping it's you, my favorite treat.
But it's not you; you're nowhere to be
found.
You're like a memory now; I don't
remember your face,
But I do remember that
I loved you when you were mine;
I loved you with every breath of mine.

The price you pay for loving the
dangerous ones
Is you never understand the difference
between toy guns—
A rubber bullet or a real one;
As they hit you, you wonder which one
it was.

And that day, as you aimed your gun at
me,
Not knowing it was real, I let it pierce
me,
Hoping I'd run to you while the shells
jabbed my feet,
As I did every time you tried to leave.

But my world slipped beneath my feet
As I fell to the ground. You tell me it's
real this time,
That the fire was put out, with only
ashes remaining,
That we're done, no more complaining.

You hated stories with open endings,
So you'd ask me every time how it
ended.
And I told you the same ending each
time:
One of them dies, one of them lives.
You believed that wasn't true;
Not every story has the same ending.
You believed in a happier conclusion,
Unaware of the law of the universe.

And when our ending came, you pushed
me down the ditch.
I was gasping for air, but I was alive,
And you left me there, at death's door.
You went on your way, satisfied you
didn't launch the final blow,
And I lay there bleeding, knowing I
would die a slow death.

———————————————

All this show had were enduring
mysteries.
Every episode consisted of unresolved
conflict.
I wrap our little cabin with the list I
made
Of all the questions you left
unanswered
And the questions you were too scared
to answer.
Every step creaks, echoing the whispers
of unsaid words;
Silence settles in the spaces where love
was supposed to thrive.

And as I write the last one, I ignite it
from the end.
It brings to the ground what you and I
thought was the endgame,
Along with the questions, burnt to a
crisp.
The wind flows in agreement, carrying
away the smoke of unresolved conflicts,
As rain pours down, the ghosts of the
past are released.

People ask me if it still hurts,
While pointing at my maimed heart.
And my impaired soul, my lack of trust.
But this wound certainly left its scar.
You're like the bruise on my arm that
only hurts when I press it,
And in that moment, all I can think
about is the excruciating pain
That used to come in waves, now
gushes towards me.
Each reminder feels like a stone thrown
at me,
These badges of survival are pinned
down on my stone cold heart.
A flicker of hope is all you need to ignite
it,
And then watch as it burns with faith,
Till only grey remains, a lifeless weak
heart.

You're unsure of whether I love you or
not,
You're uncertain of the presence of
love.
I'm terrified of heights and the ocean,
But if you were to fall from the sky into
the ocean,
I'll jump after you; I'll do everything to
save you.
You're worth every leap into the
unknown—
The black hole, the depths of the sea.
I am made brave by the love I have for
you.
This is how I know I love you.

To love is to step on a landmine, hoping
it's deactivated.
To love is to step off safely.
To love is to burst into pieces.
To love is to dance on the edge of a
blade,
To love is to trust that the wound will be
worth it.

The hourglass of my time started the
moment I closed my eyes.
History taught me that time would
never be by my side.

Everything is a ticking time bomb when
you're raised on pressure mines.
Slinking and walking on your toes, too
scared to wake up the giant,
And the mother goose with her golden
eggs.

Living in the shadows, too afraid to face
the light,
Keeping the curtains closed, a loaded
pistol by your side.
A pawn in a game of chess, always
ready to retreat,
Wearing the armour of regrets,
shielding your chest.

Because that's the way the cowards live
—
No epics written, no elegies recited.

I do not want to hurt myself, I repeat, as
I fight the urge to harm myself.
I cannot keep doing this, I repeat, as I
reach for the shiv in my drawer,
As I press it against my arm and pierce it
into my skin.
Fighting back tears, I repeat again and
again,
I do not want to hurt myself.
Gasping for air, I repeat again and again,
I cannot keep doing this to myself.
I suppress my screams; my chest
tightens,
The back of my throat hurts, my heart
becomes heavy.
I am still repeating, I do not want to
hurt myself.
'I keep doing it till I become myself, Till
my arm feels numb, till the tears stop,
Till the pain inside me dissolves.
I did not want to hurt myself, I keep
repeating.
I did not want to hurt myself.
I will not hurt myself again, I say,
As I place it on my nightstand, knowing
very well,
I will be doing this again.

You are the love of my life,
even if you're not in it anymore.
Even in your absence, you linger;
haunting every empty page of my life.

A misprint; a reminder of what once
was, now lost to the cruel whims of fate
and the author's pen.
A choice; a possibility; a back door
To revive in the upcoming chapters or
the final act of burial.

A tale of love; a lament of loss,
The frayed corners; a page still glued
together.
Spilled ink; words smudged with tears.
You exist even on the blank pages of my
life.

———————————————

Life feels like riding a bicycle these days.
I keep falling and hurting myself,
Each pedal forward, and I go down the
drain.

People often ask,
"Didn't you learn that in your
childhood?"
Childhood? The word feels like a rotten
fruit in my mouth,
One I want to spit out but fear being
called ungrateful
For all I had, the roof above my head,
And the food on my plate.

Childhood feels like a mirage, distant
and untouched,
A memory filled with drowning out my
cries.
With every fall, guilt fills my chest—
Am I still that ungrateful child?
Is it the weather? Is the storm too big
for me to handle?
Balancing on a unicycle in a circus of
expectations,
I juggle with doubt, mastering my new
ride,

Hoping luck will be on my side.

—————————————————

Whose fault is it if I tripped over
something
While running after you before you
faded?
It wasn't your fault, was it?
Running after you, it was me who fell,
Hit my head on the rock,
But you didn't look back.
Maybe you didn't hear me;
It wasn't your fault, was it?
My piercing cry was deafened by your
radiating hatred.
I cried for hours; I had no tears left.
You don't have any sympathy in you, do
you?
You weren't loved as a child,
But it wasn't your fault, was it?
You couldn't see my heart;
You were like a sharp piece of glass.
Every time I touched you, you cut me.
Every time I touched you, you hurt me.
And I did; I came close to you every
time
Till my hands were full of blood,
Till there was no place left to cut,
Till there was no skin to tear apart,
Till there was no heartbeat left.

But it wasn't your fault.
Yes, it wasn't your fault.

———————————————

You gave me a piece of your heart,
And I didn't know what to do with it.
It was beating and alive,
Everything I had never seen my heart do
before.
You tell me you love me;
I laugh at your naivety.
You tell me you miss me;
I question my existence.
I was running and running,
But I didn't know when to stop.
I was taught to run;
I wasn't told when to stop.
It is wrong to say I lived a life;
I've ducked and hid all my life.
All I did was survive this knife,
Spent my days in disguise.
Where do I put it all down,
The weight of all the words I left
unspoken,
The opportunities I left behind,
Just because I never believed something
could be mine?
I love and I love; I keep giving it away.
I fill your heart with love; I don't know
when to stop,
And suddenly you're choking on it,

And suddenly I'm back in my
abandoned cave again,
And suddenly you never come near me
again.
There is a monster of evil, and there is a
monster of good;
I'm none of them. I'm a monster of love;
I haunt you with my love.
I'm the worst kind of monster, my love.
I have a deeply unloved child in me;
She'll always be a part of me.

———————————————

How does the blood clot if the wound is
not on the flesh?
How does a wound heal when it's not
on the body?
Do tears that roll down ever form a
river?
Does the river ever lead to the wild sea?
Were my hopes a little too high?
Were the crushed dreams ever buried?
Was the grave given a tombstone?
If a person dies every day of their life,
what last date was marked on the
stone?
Is pain a part of the DNA?
Did I inherit it from my ancestors?
Was it the past that maledicted this
bloodline?
Am I the last soldier to be blown away
by my own weapon?

———————————

My birthday went dry this year.
No tears helped me set sail into
the thunderstorm of adulthood.
Tales of woe I wrote bled in
on my hands as I write the date of
today.
In choked desolation, I enter the cage of
sorrow.
Sorrow pulls me into its warm embrace,
painting me blue.
Still, my eyes were dry;
no cascade or cataract of my sadness
fell.
The unshed tears became still,
bouncing back into my eyes,
Filling the voids of my brain
until it's no longer hollow.

Everything I've ever done, I've done it
wrong.
My life didn't have a path painted out
for me;
There was no zebra crossing laid out for
me.

I had to walk blindly into the traffic,
Each honk and shout pulling me deeper
into the void,
Surrounded by the cacophony of
choices I never made.
My fairy tales became my nightmares.

Having nothing to hold onto,
No one to save me from the rush.
So I hold the hands of people who will
betray me.
Each rope they throw at me could help
me;
Each rope they throw at me could end
me.
Which rope is a lifeline and which one is
a noose?

A lost child will hold the hand of anyone
who offers,

Even the devil's himself.

I drown in the depths of my own
despair every day,
yet the surface remains calm.
I burn each day, but I don't have scars to
prove that I was lit.
My lifeboat has punctures,
the shore feels so far away.
Turbulence grips my sinking feet,
hurricanes lift my boat from the sea.
I've lived longer than most at my age,
yet I'm still seventeen, carrying a
burden that feels like a lifetime.

The hardest question you could ask me
is about my identity: who am I?
I know I have a name;
Though there are times when I forget it
as well.
If I were to tell you about myself,
I'd use two words: never enough.
I am the flower that shatters in your
hands
when you pluck it from the bush.
I am the petals you discard after
breaking the flower.
I am the mistake that taught you to pick
the next flower with care.
I am the unlucky flower, too delicate for
the hands of this world

All my life I've never been home.
Home is comfort; a warmth not made
for my heart.
I've been walking on needles,
Each needle piercing my skin as the
ground beneath me shakes.
Each step a reminder of the weight on
my shoulders and the heaviness in my
chest.
Not every rainbow has a golden pot;
Some just end in a meaningless void.
Not every cave has light at its end;
Some are shrouded in shadows, candle
dust.
Not all paths lead to a beautiful
destination;
Some lead toward a sinkhole or a ditch,
Deep enough to trap you for life.
Choices I make weigh me down the
path of despair—
Of hatred, of yearning, of longing.
Punished for dreams I dared to dream,
A punishment they should add to the
book of law:
A life sentence.

I am my mother's child.
I build dams in the lakes of my tears.
I carefully construct bridges that cannot
be crossed,
Paths to nowhere, leading to empty
spaces.

My pericardium is thicker than others,
A covering forged in the fires of fear and
sadness.
But even the strongest shields have
cracks.

I started running at the sound of the
bell,
And I've kept running since then,
Even after the race was over.
But I can't outrun the blood that runs
through these veins.

I am my mother's daughter,
Yet a complete stranger in her gaze,
A reflection of her dreams, a vessel of
failure.
I am everything she never wanted me to
be.

The gullible child never gets what they
want.
You ask for a chocolate bar, and you
leave with a candy in your hands.
You ask for a dollhouse, and you leave
with a car set,
Because it's what your big brother
wanted,
And they convinced you that it's what
you wanted,
Until you forget what you truly desire.

Although we started the same race,
My lane was barricaded,
So I had to run in his lane,
But I had only just started walking.
Halfway there, both tracks are closed.
This is as far as I can go.
I watch as he runs to the finish line,
A competition in which he stands alone.
He wins, and I'm still here, all alone.

What should I wear?
Black? Or whatever I normally wear
To the funeral of the girl I could've
been,
Of the dreams I sewed together since
forever.
What do I wear to honor the ghost of all
my potential?
How do I lay what I could've been in the
coffin?
How do I say goodbye to what I
should've been?
How do I grieve a loss of someone who
never was?
How do I look up at the sky and mourn
the future that could have been?

"We gather here to mourn the loss of a
girl and her aspirations, along with her
what-ifs."
Do I scatter petals on her grave?
Do I bury the memories within?
Perhaps I'll wear black and my usual
colors,
A tapestry of what I've lost and what I
still carry.

The hand placed on the gun starts
rotting too,
If I hold it for too long, if I stay perfectly
still.
How many times can I pretend to grab
the grip?
How many times can I check the
magazine?
The safety is off; the silencer is on,
Yet the trigger still remains untouched.
How many times can I slide my finger
away from the trigger?
How many times can I adjust it on my
sphenoid?
What is this, a coward's way out or a
brave move?
The hand is rotting now;
Yet the decision is still mine to make.

Why would you want to leave your
parents' house?
It's cold and warm, a perfect place to
live—
A warm bed and warm food,
Yet I needed to heal,
I am suffocating in this fabric of
familiarity.
A wound never heals if you keep picking
at the scab;
This house feels like salt on my wound,
an unhealed blister.
I learned to navigate life here at a
distance—
Involved in their lives, but they're not in
mine.
I live in this house but seldom leave my
room,
Talking to them about the weather,
Not the storm that rages inside me,
The cyclone that consistently hits,
Mixed emotions swirling,
The dried-up pillow in the morning
soaked with un-cried tears.

The invisible string of my fate is
strangling me,
And I keep tangling in it as I walk the
path destined for me.
I've spent my fair share of time
Blaming the sky for my cruel fate.
How much wrong can one person
commit
Till fate intervenes and rights the
wrongs?
How much bad can a person endure
Till only good remains in the world?

I walk on eggshells beneath the vast sky,
I look up at the stars and think of the
Big Guy,
Praying the next lightning doesn't strike
high,
Hoping every tear I shed will be my last
cry.
Eagerly expecting the Angel of Death
To be waiting around the next corner,
To meet the end mid-sentence, mid-
poem, mid-life.

Autopsy reports showed it was a human body,
Decaying under the ever-growing moss.
The cause of death yet to be determined,
Every organ thoroughly examined—
An astonishing case, a staggering example.
Starting from the top, the brain laid bare on the table,
Sadness embedded in parts the scientists have yet to discover.
The heart was locked in a cage, A floral pattern etched on the heart, Ripped from the chest post-mortem.
A shame we couldn't cure this person, they say,
Empathetic sighs echo through the room.
They run the blood in the DNA testing machine,
Hoping to identify this malodorous beauty—
No blood matches theirs,
Now an unidentified grave in an abandoned cemetery.

Caution signs, warning sirens,
The ticking sound at the start of the door.
You insist on going in, so I let you.
I read out all the safety instructions.
You place your first step on the floor, and it creaks.
I warn you to turn back, but you never listen.

You fall through the rotted floor,
A space no one has entered for a long time.
You seem astounded, but I told you it was the first rule.
You notice the cavity slowly filling with water
And complain about drowning.
You can't enter a broken house
And then complain when it starts to leak.

The holes are too big to cover in the time we have left together.
You leave the place. It's okay—
Just one more hole from your entrance.

How long can blood rush from the same
wound?
How long can gore be used as ink
To write the same words over and over
again,
To hide the same pain, to let it go up in
flames?
Now and then, we re-read the same
lines,
Feel the same emotions, surf through
the same tides.

We're stuck in a time loop; every day
feels like that day
When you leave, and I slam the door,
And the ground shakes like it never has
before.
The tears fall down the same way every
day—
Everything happens by the same script,
every day.
My own life is my hell loop.

Your memories, your apologies—
They are like fuel to the blazing fire
That has been burning inside me for
ages.
Every "sorry" stokes the flames of my
rage;
Every apology pours gasoline on the
blaze.

The fire that burned the human in me,
The fire that brought my courage
plummeting to the ground!
Home—that is where it all started,
Ignited by my very own hands.

Home is where the fire began,
Where it burned my soul and scattered
the ashes.
The flames bring chaos to my heart,
And the halls that haunt me go up in
smoke.

To this day, the flesh remains ablaze;
To this day, the embers persist.
You'll never be able to stop,
You'll never be able to hide:

The scars that will remind you forever
Of the start of your never-ending
misery.
Home, a furnace of my creation,
Where warmth turned to wrath.

The heat still lingers on my skin;
The ashes of my innocence scatter in
the wind.

After years of constant taunts,
Your words and eyes still haunt.
Every day I am reminded of my worth,
Since the very first day of my birth.

If you had loved me from the start,
If you knew I too had a heart,
Would you still let it be crushed?
Would you still fuel its self-disgust?

Was I made to carry your burden?
Was I just a side character?
Or do I have my own story?
You never gave me the chance;

Years have passed, yet I cannot stop
Complaining about the childhood I lost.
To protect my leftover youth,
Mother! I'm sorry, I cannot continue.

———————————

How many times can I be saved?
How much longer until it's engraved—
A medal of hurt, a painful flood,
A piece of me, my flesh and blood.

The pain rides heavy upon my back,
Tiring me down until I snap.
A rope forever wrapped 'round my
neck;
It matters not how thick the thread,
For it's either enough to asphyxiate
Or thin enough to lacerate.

Each time I grasp the lifeline, it fades,
What does salvation look like beyond
this haze?
How many hands have reached to help
me? I'll never know—
Am I the hero, or a mere spectator
In the relentless show of my pain?

The state I live in these days has many names:
Friends call it depression, doctors label it agoraphobia—
But it's neither.
My heart aches in your absence;
My mind's low on serotonin, starved of your smile.
The gloomy days have returned this month,
The atmosphere thick with sad melancholy.

Days turn into months, yet the gray air lingers,
Hours flow into the future, but you remain stuck in the past.
You blame your weary heart, but the truth is,
Every muscle in your body tires—except the heart.
The cardiac muscle does everything it can
To keep you alive, to let you live.
Yet you criticize it, wishing for its silence.

But the old heart will beat until it can't
anymore,
It will beat until the last ounce of hope.

Mom, have you ever thought about
that?
I could have been a better daughter
If you had been a better mother.
You taught me I was capable of no
good, nothing at all,
But tell me, what have you achieved?

If you were a better daughter,
Why are you not happy?
Why are you half-eaten, half-crushed?
Why do your eyes brim with anger,
Why do they spill with sadness?

Were you a perfect daughter, Mom?
Or were you a version of me?
Are you who you are, mother?
Or are you a version of your own
mother?

When my time comes, when I become a
mother,
I promise to break this cycle, to end this
curse.
I'll tell her she's good; I'll remind her
that I love her.

I'll show her she's capable of all she desires.

I will be myself; I won't be like you.
It's time for change; it's time to heal.
I'll nurture her soul; I won't shatter her heart.
I won't repeat your mistakes.
I won't do what you did.
I won't fill her with regret and guilts.

When you asked, I told you I was fine
While wondering what you would do if I
died.
Would you cry because you loved me?
Would you feel relieved because you
loved me?
Would you cry because of human
nature, or would you cry because you
loved me?
For you, I wanted to win the toy from
the claw machine.
For you, I would willingly waste all the
years of my teen.
Every time I write, it is not me; you are
my words, you are my poems.
How much do you mean to me?
Why do you mean everything to me?
Why are you the first thought in my
mind?
You will be the last thought in my mind.
If loving someone so hard would turn
you mad,
I'd be a psychopath; you'll probably be
sane.
If loving someone would pay you,
I'll be the billionaire of your heart; you'll
be a mendicant in my heart.

And if loving someone would turn your
life into colors,
I'll be the rainbow on your drawing
page;
you'll be the lifeless stickman at the end
of the page.

———————————————

You're everything I'll ever want,
You're my best deal, my 3-in-1,
You're like my favorite jacket—the one
everyone wants,
And the one I won't let anyone touch.

You're the favorite page of my life, filled
with all my best stickers.
And now you're gone, Just like that,
Nowhere to be found.
You slipped away in open sight, You put
up a good fight.

Now I have to restart my life, Rewind all
our good times,
Make myself forget your scent,
Take away all the colors I saw you
wearing.

Because it hurts—it's way too painful.
It hurts so much, I don't know how to
tell you.
The word "hurt" is nothing compared to
what you made me feel.
The word "love" is nothing compared to
what I felt for you.

All this care, and you chose to go.
All this love, but you chose to leave.
Tell me, is love ever enough?

I wasn't loved enough—it left a hole in
my chest.
You were loved way too much—you're
still in a state of unrest.

You brought all the colors into my black-
and-white life.
You're gone now, and I'm back to being
blind.
I don't have any seasons in my life
anymore,
I don't have beautiful sights in my life
anymore.

I look in the mirror, and I'm not there.
I look around, and you're not there.
I punch the walls, hoping to move the
planet,
With all this rage for you—but you're
not here.
With all this love for you—but oh God,
you're not here.

It's 6 a.m., and I must get ready for
college.
I dress up, eat the breakfast I made
myself,
and get on the bus, thinking the same
thing I do every day:
"I do not want to return home again."

When I come back, Mother is cooking in
the kitchen.
I enter, and she is crying.
She is crying, but she is cutting onions.
I ask, "Are you crying, Mother?"
"No, dear. I'm cutting onions," she
replies.

She is cutting onions, I tell myself.

Later, she says she has to buy some
things
and gets ready to go.
I resume cutting the onions, trying to
help.
They are sweet onions—the green ones,
with less sulfur, less pungency.
They don't make you cry. I know that,
Mother.

I'm a medical student, remember?
You made me choose it.
You wanted me to be a doctor.

If the onions were sweet, then what
was making you cry?

You have a good marriage.
It can't be work—you love your job.
Is it your failed daughter? Is it me,
Mother?

But I'm doing medicine for you.
I sit like a woman should, I laugh like a
woman should.
Please, don't be more disappointed in
me.

I am not well, dear Mother.
I am ill.
I don't feel well mentally or emotionally.
But you don't understand,
and I don't tell you anything anyway.

I am capable of nothing. I am
depressed.
I have been this way since I was eight.

You called me a fool for being like this.

So I killed myself—the real me.
I am now a fake figure, just as you
wanted me to be.
I am interested in makeup and
hairstyles,
and how to make myself prettier,
like a woman should be.

I am everything you wanted me to be.
I am nothing I wanted myself to be.

I may very well be an accomplished
doctor someday—
with fair skin and a pretty face,
a body that fits into the clothes
you bought for younger me,
the ones I was too big to fit into.

I may very well be all those things,
Mother.
But I must tell you one thing:

I may never be happy again.
No, I will never be happy again.

Why can't I copy what I'm feeling onto
this notebook?
Why are the words I write not as
powerful as my pain?
The page begins to burn as I write about
you,
and the pen's tip keeps breaking, over
and over again.

It makes me wonder—if I told you
everything,
would you also burn? Would you also
break?
Could you endure the weight of my
rage,
or would you shatter on the very first
page?

You ask how I write such heartbreaking
poetry—
but could you handle the truth that it's
all about you and me?

But I won't do to you what you did to
me.
I won't rip out your heart and toss it
aside.

I'll keep writing, I'll keep burning the
pages.
I'll keep breaking the pen, and I'll keep
suffering.

Because I love you—and that's my curse
to bear.
I won't let you taste the medicine you
once gave me

A withered flower doesn't bloom again,
no matter how much love you pour into
it,
no matter how hard the rain falls over
it.
It's too late—the flower grew tired
of waiting to be noticed by you,
hoping, always hoping, to be seen by
you.

So why should I believe you now?
Why did you think I'd still be here
waiting?
It's not that you were wrong—
it's that you were right.

I'm still here, with all my petals laid
bare,
still here, waiting for you.
You came to me only when you missed
me,
never caring about the nights I longed
for you,
the moments I ached for you.

And yet, I remain.

I hate myself for it, but it doesn't
change a thing.
So come now—chain me.
Make me beg for your love once more.
Make me fall for you all over again.

I'll never feel whole again,
A part of me will always be with you.
Unlike a worm, I won't be able to
regenerate—
Would you come back before it's too
late?

Drowning in the pool of my own tears,
Staring as reality weighs down on me.
I'll have to row the boat alone—or jump
off.
Would it really be my fault to abandon a
sinking ship?
Or should I go down with it, as the
elders say?

And I'll have to shed my skin, like a
snake,
To rid myself of you, along with all this
filth
They dare to call love.

I wish I were the water drops
condensed on your bathroom mirror,
After a hot shower that made you feel
better.
I wish I were the ray of sunlight falling
on your face,
Through half-drawn curtains at 8 in the
morning.

I wish I were your superhero alarm
clock,
Resting by your bedside, waking you up
every time.
I wish I were the termite gnawing away
at the wood in your closet,
Quiet, unnoticed, yet always there.

I wish I were that old grocery receipt,
folded in your wallet,
The one you never got around to
throwing out.
I wish I were the star you stared at a
second longer than the others on your
walk home,
Because it shined the brightest.

I wish I were the clovers growing in the
cracks beneath your doorstep,
The ones you step over without a
glance, every single day.

Your love is like residual heat, mother,
It reignites me now and then—
Every time I'm done with life,
Every time my fire starts to dim.

You hug me, mother,
Just when I'm about to lose my grip.
You grab the rope; you pierce it into my skin
You make sure it hurts, ensuring I feel every bit.

Surely, there must be an end.
Surely, my life isn't a dead end.
There must be a purpose—
A story I've missed along the way.
But I'll never have the chance.

Look, mother, just like you said:
I'm a lost cause, a use to no one.
Who would love a broken daughter?
Who would love a living horror?

The rain might have washed out the
fire,
But it's not cold yet.
I could rekindle the flame, revive my
heart—
But I don't want that just yet.

The sun shines brighter than ever now,
My wings are melting as I soar too high,
Higher than the sky, though the sky was
the limit.
I didn't learn the lesson of Icarus.
And now I've fallen—perished, or
perhaps punished.

But if the world were ending, I'd do it all
again.
I'd walk on bare stones, I'd lay on
burning sand.
I'd search for purpose and find my way
through.
I'd take the leap of faith and risk it all.

In my second chance, I won't play it
safe.
I'll risk a broken heart,
And stare at the sky with swollen eyes.

I won't live cautiously—
I'd rather have a heart than a block of
ice.

I won't just survive.
I'll live

———————————————

It's always my fault,
It's always my fault.
Don't bother finding the clues,
Don't bother solving the puzzles.

The signs and signals might only deceive
you—
I cover my tracks as I walk further down
the street.
I always keep my side of the street
clean,
So no need to wear your best detective
hat.

I apologize for the inconvenience my
existence has caused you,
I apologize for any offense.
I'm just a very sorry human being.
I'd say sorry to anyone, except the
mirror.

My street is a loop I walk every day,
And I always end up in front of myself.
I'm always the one to blame—
Both sides of the street are mine.

People often tell you to bury your past,
Move on with your life, bury the
hatchet.
But my earth isn't big enough to bury it
all.
My mistakes and regrets can't be
covered
By the dirt of this world.

I'd still have to walk on the pointy soil of
my past,
Risk bruising my feet on the shards of
old memories.
Things you bury don't stay buried—
They grow.
And my soil has the perfect nutrient for
mistakes: Guilt.

My past sprouts roots in my future,
Until it surrounds me from all four sides.
And there I am,
Sitting with my past at 3 in the morning.
Unable to remember what I have been
fighting for this long.

Uncovering the truth behind the lies,
I walk, burning the bridges behind me.
They warn me I'll need them in time,
But I don't need a road; I won't go back
there again,
Not under their watchful eyes and
judgmental sighs.

I'm leaving behind this masquerade,
Worn out from dressing as a clown
And joining the circus they call life.
The city lights burn through my eyes,
A chart of my good and bad deeds,
Written in my own blood.

Carrying the burden of every gaze that
fell upon me,
I don't know how to finish a poem,
But I do know how to finish my life.

A single smear of paint ruins the whole
portrait.
A small flaw, a careless stroke—and now
you've ruined what could've been a
masterpiece.
But every masterpiece created is now
stored in a box, with a fragile sticker on
top.

Can beauty remain untouched?
Even mountains are drilled through
their hearts in search of something
more.
Perfection is a myth we keep digging for,
in the chests of those closest to us.

I am not perfect because I am not
meant to be perfect.
So why is everyone chasing perfection—
something that doesn't exist?

———————————

Give me the pieces of your broken
heart.
These so-called pathetic fragments,
they're not pathetic; they're lovable.
Perhaps what your heart needs is a
friend,
someone to treat it gently.
After all, this is its first time beating.
I'll try to mend these pieces of yours;
I promise you that.
And if the pieces don't fit together,
I'll join my pieces with yours.
Together we'll create a new heart,
a new heart that beats.
And I'll give it to you, just as I said.
You deserve this thing in red,
but you'll have to promise me
you'll take care of it, you'll let it beat.
It's not just your heart; it's ours,
so let it beat for my sake.
As for me, I don't need a heart—
a heart is meant to love people,
and I have failed in this task:
to love, or to be loved.

If history could be rewritten,
If things were given a different ending,
If I had known you wouldn't show
mercy,
If I had known your heart was too cruel
for that

If I knew I'd spend the rest of my life in
tears,
If I knew you'd never be by my side—

I still would have fallen in love with you.
I'd have gone through the heartbreak all
over again.
I'd have loved you just the same,
And let you play with my heart all over
again

Even if the sirens had gone off
Even if every word was a blade I
disguise
I wouldn't have changed this story
You were the only chapter worth writing

I wouldn't have loved you any less,
And I still wouldn't have thought of
myself.

I never believed in fairytales, until I met
you.
You were my Prince Charming, but I saw
the Beast in you.
I didn't have the best first impression,
I didn't even notice you at first glance,
Yet somehow, you read me right
through.

I was lost in my fantasies, drifting away
from reality.
I knew my dreams weren't real, yet I
clung to them.
I pushed you away, not because of you
—
The roses I walked past always wilted
and dried.
Bad luck was my friend, like a shadow
close by.

The beautiful smile you wore—I
couldn't bear to ruin it too.
The sparkle in my eyes wasn't always
real;
My pillow knows the truth behind the
glitter.

I've been trouble all along.
You've been through your share too—
Two broken souls, could we have made
it through?

If only my breaths had stopped before
yours,
We would have known a different
ending,
But good times never last—they slip
away too soon.

Maybe in another life, maybe on a
softer day,
Our paths will cross, and we'll find a
way.
Until then, may we meet again
someday.

———————————

The easy child, the family clown,
The one everyone laughs at,
The one who is never taken seriously.
How hard it is to live in this skin,
When you don't fit in anyone's life—
The vestigial organ of the family,
The experiment child, the first draft,
Tested, reshaped, molded, and wielded,
Then left out in the cold, watching
through the window
As the fog accumulates on it.
Watching them live while I freeze to
death.
The black sheep, the outsider in the
family alliance,
Bad blood flows through my veins—
unacceptable blood.
The forgotten child, the outgrown child.
But as long as the appendix doesn't
burst, no one removes it.
As long as I stay quiet, maybe I'll have a
chance
To be a part of this family.

Did you ever get tired from constantly
highlighting my flaws?
Did you ever see who I really was?
Did you ever meet your daughter,
or was I just another expired product?

Mom, you made me feel like a wrongly
shaped thing—
the kind they send to cheap stores,
sold at much cheaper rates.

Dad, you treated me like a doll—
a doll without a heart or a brain.
I was there. I was your daughter.
I am your daughter. You made me.

You were supposed to raise me,
but you ate me alive.

I could not be the perfect daughter,
but I was still yours. I was yours,
but you were never mine.

I was there, but you never saw me.
You saw someone who wasn't me.
That wasn't me, Father.

This is me now.
You really molded me into a wrongly
shaped product,
but instead of selling me cheaply,
I was sent to be destroyed—
such a bad piece that no one would
want,
not even for free.

Now they will kill me and recycle me for
a better life.

In the next life, I hope I don't end up
with you.
Families are supposed to be special—
so, God, why is mine a nightmare?

But I can't hate you. I can't.
I don't want to lose you,
and I don't seem able to change that.
You are my parents— the only truly
loved relationship.

If this is love, then please, hate me.
but don't burn me alive with your love.

Am I that bad? Am I that flawed?

Why do you think God created me?
Did He want me to be the most hated
creature?
Did He want to see how many flaws
He could place in one person?

Who should I complain to, Mother ?
Who should I hug, Father?

———————————————

Since you've said goodbye, the moon no
longer rises in my city.
I've spent lifetimes waiting, but without
you, time refuses to pass.
I've tried to love again, but my heart
doesn't beat like it did for you.
I've bowed in prayer, whispered every
wish,
but the truth is, not everyone gets their
wish.
In the wind, I hear the silence fly, but
time stands still for no one..
My heart often chooses the alleyways of
sorrow,
but for this lost wanderer, no road
awaits.
The sun rises each day just as bright;
the world's rhythm doesn't stop for
anyone's absence.
And whom should I complain to?
This world has never been on my side.
I know it's partly my fault;
I have always ignore what people say;
what they warn.
Now, there's a broken home, a broken
road—

but that's my destination, the path that
once led there.
When it's too late, words lose their
meaning;
a withered flower holds no worth.
When I want to speak, it feels as if
a dagger lies lodged in my throat.
With my final breath, I have lived for
you,
and with my final breath, I'd died for
you.

You were so naive, little me,
to believe someone would truly love
you,
just for the way you are.
Your own mother doesn't love you
for the way you are.
Your very flesh reminds her of what you
are—
a terrible result, a sorry excuse of a
human,
a blunder, a failure, a fiasco.

Did you really think the world was
beautiful?
That there was light at the end of the
cave,
a pot of gold at the end of the rainbow?
You were so naive, little me,
to think that maybe one day
your mother would be proud,
proud that her blood runs through your
veins.
You wanted to prove them wrong,
to show them you were capable of
amazing things.
Tell me now, were they right, or were
they wrong?

You're still naive, my friend,
thinking someone would accept you
just for the way you are,
thinking you still have a chance.

You're fooling yourself.
You always have been.
You'll never change, love.

The knife isn't far,
the light is nearly gone,
and time has ended.
"She was so naive," they said,
as they let go of me and my pain,
wrapped in white, never to be touched
again.
"She was so young," they said.

The ghost of my childhood paid me a
visit today,
when I went on vacation to the same
place I did at six.
It's a whole different world, but the
same old nostalgia.
I walk the paths my younger self once
did,
feeling like a time traveler opening
doors
in the museum of my memory.

And there she is—sitting in a corner,
the last place I left her whole,
before life chiseled away her innocence.
I see her laughing, running,
and I weep at the thought
of how disappointed she would be
to learn where we ended up in time,
to hear how life treated us.

I stand before her, both proud and
regretful.
"She's all I ever want to be," we say,
gazing into each other's eyes.

Today, I decided to tidy up my room,
to take out the things that no longer
have a place in my life.
Little did I know I was inviting grief in for
dinner,
but I knew grief loves to overstay its
welcome.
An unwelcome visitor,
grief moves into my house,
occupying every corner of my room
and slipping into the drawers of my
cupboards.

I open the box of unfulfilled dreams,
dust collecting on top,
overflowing with my lost potential—
who I could have been, should have
been.
Grief follows me around the room,
clinging to my barely holding-together
heart.
I close the box again,
leaving these unprocessed feelings for
another time.

The wind of despair flows through my
tied-up hair,
I sit near the lake of distress,
Watching as the waves crash; fish
resign.
Time flees by, marking the loss of my
life.

I am not made for life-altering adversity,
Nor for the rigors and asperity of the
hunters.
A piece unfit to complete the puzzle,
Always searching for something greater.

Sorry for my loss, but also for all I have
to gain—
Sorrow and grief, growing old, the cycle
of life.
The philosophy of existence and the
way it ends,
A poet's deepest, darkest desire.

All they had to give and all that was
taken away,
The greatest desire: rest for our weary
bodies
And immortality for our words.

AUTHOR'S NOTE

Writing this book has been a journey through memories, dreams and unspoken thoughts. This book is a dream come true for me. I have wanted a published book out there written by me ever since I was a kid. Each poem holds a piece of my heart and this collection was born from the ache of feeling too much.

Thank you, dear reader, for opening these pages and reading these words that hold my heart.
An honorary mention to my friends-Huda, Laiba, Yashal & Moizza- without whom this book would never have existed.

CONTACT:-
@eventhemoonwrites on Instagram
Email: eventhemoonwrites@gmail.com